THE ART OF MYSTICISM

Practical Guide to Mysticism & Spiritual Meditations

Gabriyell Sarom

Contents

Publications

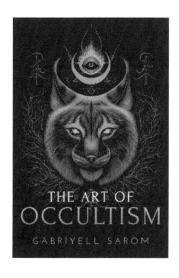

The Art of Occultism

The Secrets of High Occultism &
Inner Exploration

The Art of Magick

The Mystery of Deep Magick &
Divine Rituals

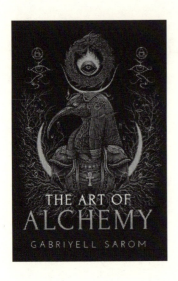

The Art of Alchemy

Inner Alchemy & the Revelation of the
Philosopher's Stone

**Subscribe to Gabriyell Sarom's
Newsletter and receive the book:**

*Divine Abilities:
3 Techniques to Awaken Divine Abilities*

www.sacredmystery.org

Dedication

This book is dedicated to all students of Mysticism searching for a path back towards God.

Introduction

From the beginning of time, curiosity has led mankind to question their surroundings. In the search to understand life, the universe, the psyche, consciousness, and God, humans were also inevitably led to question themselves and their own existence.

In seeking to respond to those perennial enigmas and find freedom from sorrow to pursue lasting happiness, some rare humans encountered a deep source of wisdom, realizing that there was something besides their mere five senses.

The presence of enlightened mystics in different eras and nations led all those who sought this source of wisdom, quietude, and freedom to follow them and learn how to decode this transcendental mystery, thus beginning a journey in search of the sacred mystical knowledge and realization to unveil what lies beyond.

This is a book centered on mystical practices that make such a discovery possible. Theory will be employed, but to a minimal degree and only when it is required. We don't want to waste anyone's time on doctrine and beliefs. Here the reader will find detailed mystical practices and meditations that will assist in establishing a suitable mystical routine, from the basic setup to the most advanced practice by which a student can accomplish the ultimate godly realization. All students are welcome, from the most inexperienced to the most advanced.

The instructions contained in this book intend to provide a shortcut to the divine, and not a diversion of the student's attention to the satisfaction of sensual pleasures in the physical and subtle planes. This is why we will not attempt to satisfy the intellectual mind of a casual onlooker and fulfill its longings for the knowledge of useless but fancy practices or mental abilities that lead to nowhere. They do not bring Godly union and legitimate mystical wisdom. However, the physical embodiment of the divine is relevant, and that will be addressed.

We sincerely hope the reader enjoys this work and that it may serve as the fertile ground from which the divine tree of mystic wisdom can grow back towards its perennial source.

SECTION 1

Unraveling Mysticism

1

The Goal of Mysticism

First and foremost, mysticism is Union with God. A definition of mysticism could not be both meaningful and comprehensive enough to include all sorts of experiences or realizations which have been described as "mystical". Ergo, rather than giving multiple definitions besides "Union with God", we will let students find their own definition through the first-hand experience of the divine.

Most people believe that mysticism is the discipline of acquiring supernatural or divine abilities. These abilities may be of great use, but they are secondary in the mystical journey. Students should always seek the supreme, God, and only afterwards will such divine abilities be bestowed upon them with the necessary training and spiritual merit. These mystical abilities will be one of the many outcomes of the consequent integration of the gained realization into one's own life.

Only through practice, study, and application of the principles shared by realized Masters can mysticism be unraveled. This implies that a persevering student can achieve this realization of Union with God given sufficient practice and sincere surrender to the method and goal. This merging is verily the goal of the mystic.

2

The Superior Path

any are the comparisons made between mysticism and religion, with some defining the two as the same thing, but there are clear differences. It is in this sense that we will here expose their differences to clarify the reader.

In the majority of religions, all of the answers are given to their followers. These answers are accepted as absolute truth without necessarily having first-hand experience into that supposed truth. This belief-based knowledge is not the type of teaching that we want to accentuate in this work.

Many devotees of these religions develop an unshakeable faith in their religion and its teachings, becoming highly conditioned and blind. In religion, authority is in the third person. It is never in the student's first-hand experience.

This belief-based religious methodology has led many devotees astray in the past.

Although some followers of these religions do have "religious experiences" or "religious ecstasies" through moments of intense prayer, this is very rare. In these rare instances, they sense the presence of God, but as a rule, it is very recurrent to go the whole life without a single glimpse of something beyond.

It is good to be a skeptic, and never should students accept the validity of a statement without having experienced that truth first.

Fortunately, the truth is both only one and timeless and has survived over the ages. Due to the blessings of some rare enlightened beings, the divine teachings go on and on, helping humanity expand its consciousness towards new unseen grandiosity.

However, because of the doctrinaire approach that prevailed, many were led to the abandonment or even disbelief in God. God became a complete act of faith and worship. But God is not truly a person living in the sky. God is indescribable, and it is up to the student to get to know Him through first-hand experience instead of reading or hearing about Him. God doesn't require any faith or worship but recognition and experience.

Mysticism is the return to God, and the highest goal of a student of mysticism is to be One with God. Then, they become a mystic.

In this way, the mystic adept is distinguished from the religious devotee by having first-hand experience as the master, transcending the need for intermediaries. This makes mysticism a superior path.

3

The Mystery of God

Since distant times humanity ascribed to the divine, to God, what they couldn't grasp or figure out. Then, they would wonder, "What is God?" Few are those who are truly able to answer this question with accuracy.

The problem appears when students create diverse interpretations of what was written in these ancient scriptures without having any direct knowledge of what God is or is not. God is completely beyond human understanding, and approaching Him through mental understanding and logic will never yield adequate results.

This recognition does not come easily, and we must go on a mystical journey until we are mature enough to absorb it through first-hand experience. This journey aims to facilitate the maturing of the mind so that it can realize its union with God.

God can appear in the form of Light, a Master, an Angel, a Deva, etc., or as any single entity or even several entities. They can all represent God. Some defend a God with a human figure; others with a figure with anatomical parts of animals.

Despite the differences between the form that God can take from student to student, this does not mean that God is different. All of the symbology and image that God represents is intended to communicate a message to the student. The image that God assumes is so that the student can easily interpret the message, so God assumes the image of something that the aspirant knows and will comprehend. This allows the student to establish a relationship with God.

Nevertheless, God is ultimately without shape, image, or limitations. It is this ultimate unspeakable that each student must get to know through the mystical path.

4

The Initiation

Initiation is generally assumed to be the foundation of mysticism: a ceremonial event with a symbolic purification, sacred vows, and an energy transmission from the Master to the student. These are done physically, and they can be a beautiful and unforgettable moment in the student's life. Their importance and role still hold true to this day.

Nonetheless, something more profound and close to the student is when they unexpectedly feel something beyond the physical senses. These experiences are undeniable, and they bring to light what is normally occult. This is the true origin of the word *mysticism*: an initiation into the occult. Although there are abundant ritualistic practices to initiate a student on the path of becoming united with God, the authentic initiation is when such an experience takes place. This is the inception of the real mystical path. Until such mystical experience, it is solely a question of belief, faith, hope, or trust in your Master, in his words, or in what books or figures of authority have said.

However, nothing profound and lasting will happen if the student doesn't practice, which is why we stress its importance. If the reader had to take one thing from this book, it would be: put all spiritual and mystical words into practice and give the most sincere efforts to achieve the supreme goal of mysticism. Armchair mystics are everywhere. But it is the genuine student that becomes a true mystic. Don't waste any time and get ready to dive deep into the rabbit hole of mysticism. It will be the most mysterious but rewarding journey of all.

5

The Pineal Gland

he pineal gland is intimately connected to mystical realization and higher levels of consciousness, and is energetically used in many mystical practices. Unfortunately, due to abnormal and superficial breathing habits and a materialistic lifestyle (among other reasons), the pineal gland has shrunken in most human beings.

As humanity has become increasingly obsessed with consumerism and capitalism, neglecting spirituality and mysticism, the pineal gland has slowly atrophied. This deterioration coincides with a progressive disregard for the vital force and conscious breathing.

Instead of basing reality only in accordance with the perception of the five limited gross senses, the student will connect with the subtler dimensions and levels of consciousness of this multi-dimensional universe.

By practicing breathing-based techniques involving the pineal gland, the nervous system, and the brain, the pineal gland will "regenerate" and metaphysically open. An advanced student of mysticism will always have a healthy and spiritually open pineal gland.

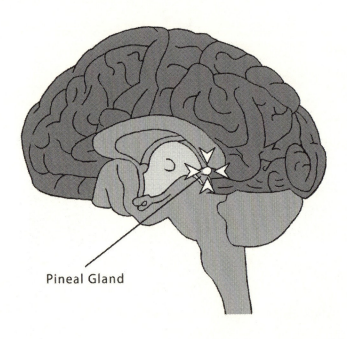

Pineal Gland

6

The Multi-Dimensional Universe

he majority of humans comprehend, perceive, and relate to the world primarily through the five physical senses.

Humans usually consider that which is perceivable to be what is real. They accept without question what their senses provide and consider them faultless. Modern science is based on these sensory faculties. Of course, the physical world does seem solid because the people who perceive it do it through physical senses (eyes, tongue, ears, etc.). Humanity puts so much emphasis on what is physically perceivable that everything that does not conform to one or more of the five physical senses is treated as an illusion or merely as imagination.

An entirely materialistic view of the world usually makes people live from an utterly consumerist perspective.

As a result, most people try to gather as much money and material possessions as possible during life in order to increase their levels of satisfaction and pleasure, and prompted by the immature mind's desire to keep up a favorable social status among peers, succumb to its unenlightened will.

Although humanity has always perceived the Universe as having three dimensions and mostly being full of "dead matter", that is only a tiny facet of the whole Cosmos. The Universe is alive, conscious, and is a multi-dimensional reality.

As a matter of fact, the Universe has much subtler dimensions than the world of physical matter. It extends beyond the perceptions of the five gross senses. The majority of the Cosmos exists at levels of vibration beyond what the five senses can perceive and outside the limits of modern scientific instruments. Although humans can seldom perceive these subtler dimensions, they are as real as this world that is seen by our eyes. These subtler dimensions are known as "astral worlds", and they are much vaster than the physical universe, populated by billions of the most varied beings.

What is external (physical universe) is perceived through the five gross senses, and what is internal (subtle or astral universe) is perceived with the mind (internal vision, internal hearing, etc.).

In this world, a person hears with their ears and sees with their eyes. In an inner world, a person hears and sees with their mind, exactly like in a dream, in a trance, or while imagining.

To the conscious human mind anchored in physicality, the physical universe seems more stable than the astral universe because the latter is more subject to rapid fluctuations or change.

To have access to the inner universe, students must have unlocked multiple mind layers that prevent them from consciously accessing such subtler dimensions. The physical senses are presently blocking the beauty and magic of the vast inner worlds, but everyone can access them with the correct mystical practice.

In fact, the physical universe comprises approximately 1% of the whole Cosmos. The other 99% are subtler than physical matter, imperceptible to the gross human senses or current scientific instruments.

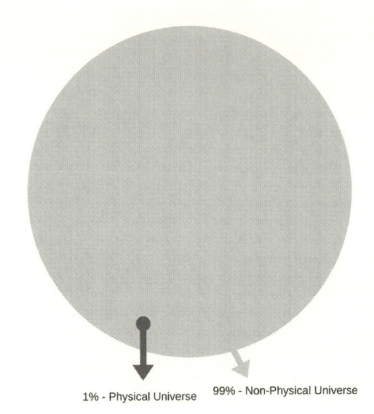

1% - Physical Universe   99% - Non-Physical Universe

In these inner worlds, it is entirely possible to communicate non-verbally with other forms of life. Some of those beings are close to this physical dimension, while others are far, far away. Nonetheless, the only barrier between both dimensions is the self-constraints imposed by one's own mind and its seductive physical senses. Many of these inner beings will help the student in the mystic path, while others not so much. The student's energy and intentions dictate the degree and purity of such encounters.

Irrespective of what we write here, the best and only way to truly comprehend and realize these facets of our multi-dimensional universe is to experience them directly through mystical practice.

SECTION 2

The Ladder Towards God

7

Mystical Practice

This is the most important chapter of this manual. These mystical practices will propel the student to be one with God if they go all the way.

Whether the student is young or elderly, with much or little experience, the key to success in mysticism lies with practice. It is unnecessary to be absent from activity or "life" to meditate the whole day. The student merely has to practice with surrender, intention, and persistence. With sufficient practice, the mystical state that occurs during the practice will extend to daily activities and life.

One of the problems many students have is that they only exercise their intellect. They think they have to know all the theory in order to practice. But that's incorrect. Anyone can start practicing right off the bat. The wisdom regarding mysticism, consciousness, God, the Universe, etc., will come as the student practices through first-hand experience.

Cultivating the habit of mystical practice

The mind has an innate tendency to maintain habits. By specifying a time to do something every day, the mind will develop the habit of automatically doing that at that time of the day. Therefore, if we practice every day at the same time of the day, in the same location, and with the same posture, the outcome will be that the mind and the body will naturally and spontaneously adjust to the peaceful and natural meditative state of consciousness just by going to practice. It will become a trained reflex and it will be tremendously easier to concentrate at this time than at any other.

Note: Never should these practices be done if the student is excessively sleepy or tired, or after eating a large meal.

Phase One: Attention

All mystical practices are nothing but consciously choosing where to put our attention and maintaining it there. Ergo, it is fundamental to know how to direct the attention to anything we might desire.

Although the process of attention is the same, it varies slightly according to what kind of object we are paying attention to. In this phase, we will learn how to place our attention in five different ways:

a) On the body.

b) On the breath.

c) On an object.

d) On a sound.

e) On space.

Before starting with the main practice, the student should do one preliminary exercise:

Close your eyes and mentally count backwards from 100 to 0. If you miss a number or lose your attention to any other thought, start over again.

As soon as you manage to do it once, you can proceed to do it five times in a row. When you succeed at this preliminary attention-based practice, you can move on to the main practice instructions.

Procedure:

a) Focus on the body

1. Wherever you are reading this right now, notice how your attention is focused on these words. Now, focus your attention on your hands. Put down the book, if required, and try your best to move your attention to your hands. Let them up in the air and notice the fuzzy tingling sensations that occur.

2. If you still don't feel anything in your hands, rub them vigorously with your fingers together for 30 seconds.

3. Notice the heat and the tingling in your hands. Focus there. See how your awareness permeates your hands.

4. Afterwards, move your attention to the feet. Notice how it feels. Try to move it to the head and other body parts. See how each point feels. Notice that there are parts of your body that you were never aware of.

b) Focus on the breath

1. Instead of breathing unconsciously and automatically, become aware of the breath.

2. Notice each inhalation and all the accompanying sensations, and each exhalation and all the accompanying

sensations. Notice the pauses between each inhalation and exhalation and between each exhalation and inhalation.

3. Maintain the focus on the breath and its fresh sensations during the inhalation and its warmer sensations during the exhalation.

c) Focus on an object

1. Choose an external object. It can be anything you desire, but the simpler, the better, such as the flame of a candle, a pen, a chair, the letter A, the Om symbol, etc.

2. Fix your gaze intensely on the chosen object. See all its visual details. Withdraw your awareness from all the other visual objects. The gaze should be focused yet tranquil. This practice must not cause stress, otherwise, it will not be beneficial. The purpose is merely to learn how to consciously use our attention and maintain it in a single point.

3. Next, close your eyes and vividly imagine the chosen object. Try your best to visualize the object with as much realism as possible. If it vanishes from your mind, try to recall it again.

Even if the mental image of the object lasts only for a few seconds, try once more.

For this exercise, visualization is imagination; there is no difference at all. When you imagine something, you don't actually "see" anything with your "eyes" or "visually", but it is like you can see without seeing, even the most delicate details.

However, if you actually see "visuals", then you are seeing with your inner sight (third eye), and it is a wonderful ability. It is not required, and all students can awaken it with sufficient practice.

d) Focus on a sound

1. Close your eyes and imagine the sound of a clock ticking noisily. Make the auditory imagination seem as realistic as possible, as if you had a real clock near you.

2. Every time you miss a few clock ticks, you should restart. Do not overdo it, or your mind might become agitated.

e) Focus on space

We can also practice our attention without what is considered to be a normal meditation object.

1. Look straight into the space in front of you with your eyes wide open. Notice the sense of space. Your vision will become slightly blurred or out of focus.

2. Without too much effort, notice that you are not focusing on any particular point but on the all-pervading space.

3. Do not become distracted by whatever occurs in your field of vision. Do not let the mind become torpid or wander. Allow your attention to perceive space rather than ignoring it as usual.

Schedule:

Do it as many times a day as you wish. At least twice. You can perform one exercise until you master it before proceeding to the next one, or you can do one after the other in the same session.

Repeat these exercises until you can:

a) Fully move your attention to any part of your body with ease.

b) Stay aware of the breath for at least 10 minutes without any distractions.

c) Maintain the visualization vividly in the inward eye for at least 30 seconds, unceasingly.

d) Continuously maintain the sound of the clock ticking for 3 minutes.

e) Be aware of the space around you, effortlessly, as if your awareness spread throughout that space.

Possible obstacles:

There are countless impediments in this practice. The primary and most recurrent impediment is losing conscious attention. The mind will start wandering off, and your focus will be distracted by worries, thoughts, etc.

The "Focus on an object" practice might seem extremely hard at first, but remember that you do not need to see the object exactly as you see with your eyes. You must see it with your mind.

Remember the door of your house. See how you can quickly and vividly see it in your mind with your internal sight. It was easy, and you just had to remember it. Try to apply the same effortlessness to the exercise.

Remember this is just a preparatory exercise, but a really important one. Do not fumble around.

The result:

After this practice, the student will know how to move the attention to any particular body part and maintain it in the breath or in any object, sound or even space. It is a basic introduction to becoming conscious of focused attention. Attention, alongside relaxation, are the two most important foundational aspects of practical mysticism.

Diluting the mind with thoughts dilutes the mind's effectiveness.

The ability to have the mind fixed on only one "thing" is one of the most essential abilities the student can develop. A single focused thought is extremely powerful. Most other mystical abilities rely on this stable attention. Without competent powers of concentration, nothing valuable can be attained. Focused attention makes the mind more serene, alert, and lucid and opens it up to go deeper into profound levels of consciousness.

Optional "Focus on the Breath" Practice:

When the student manages to hold their attention on the breath for at least 5 minutes uninterruptedly, by performing the procedure of "Focus on the breath", they can practice the *Mystic Breath*.

The Mystic Breath

The Mystic Breath is an outstanding aid for all mystical practices that utilize the breath as a meditation aid or focus. It has proven to be a great help to all those who resort to it, calming their mind, reducing the amount of mental chaos, lowering the heart rate and the metabolism by lengthening the breath, helping the body reach a deep state of relaxation with extreme ease, thus relieving accumulated tensions and so on and so forth.

The Mystic Breath can also aid the student in perceiving

the flow of the vital force coursing through the body.

The soothing sound, pressure, and vibrations make it the perfect preliminary practice. It is a useful tool always ready to be utilized by the student in all situations.

This type of breathing produces a very characteristic oceanic sound, and for that reason, many different traditions call it the breath of the ocean.

To produce this sound and this vibration, it is sufficient to constrict the back of the throat lightly while inhaling or exhaling. However, we will present more detailed instructions, which will allow the student to learn how to do it.

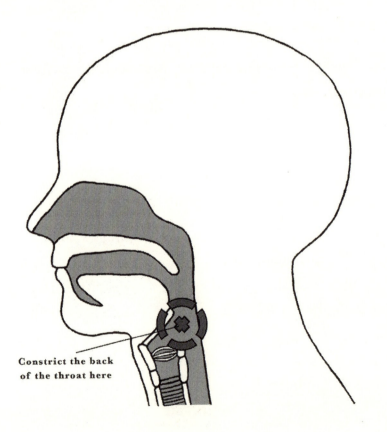

Constrict the back
of the throat here

Technique:

1. Open your mouth and expel the air as if you were fogging up a mirror.

2. Repeat the same type of exhalation by placing the hand extended in front of the mouth. Pay particular attention to the warm air touching your hand.

3. Repeat the exhalation but with the mouth closed. Exhale through the nostrils.

4. Next, inhale while maintaining the contraction of the epiglottis. It will make a similar sound to the sound of the exhalation.

5. Fully breathe while maintaining the back of the throat contracted at all times.

Below, we will share a meditation to practice the Mystic Breath.

Procedure:

1. Sit in a natural and comfortable position, without having a back support, so that you can smoothly perceive the flow of the vital energy.

2. Do five deep breaths to soothe the body and mind.

3. Begin doing the Mystic Breath for 10 to 20 minutes. Enjoy the pleasurable sensations that the Mystic Breath produces in your body.

4. After finishing, remain in your current posture and enjoy the feelings and sensations in your body. See how much calmer, peaceful and joyful you are.

Phase Two: Bodily Illumination

Body-awareness is a necessary acquisition for the student.

Procedure:

1. Sit comfortably with crossed legs or in a straight-backed chair. Find an enjoyable position and stay there. If your physical health does not allow you to sit still like that, you can prop yourself up in bed in a semi-upright posture using pillows. As a last resort, you can lie flat with your back in your bed, but make sure you do not fall asleep.

2. Observe your body, its sensations, pains, numbness, aches, tinglings, etc. Do not attempt to relax. That will be an effort that you should avoid at this moment. Do not physically move either, and do not attempt to breathe rhythmically or to watch your breathing process. Allow the mind to float free.

3. Maintain your awareness in the body and in all of the sensations that appear. Make no voluntary movement of either the body or the mind except for focusing on the body and all its sensations. Countless different sensations will emerge. Uncontrollable itches will appear for no apparent cause. Merely keep watching them to the best of your ability.

If your body-awareness starts to expand, or if it feels like your body has sunk into the ground or enlarged like a balloon, do not label, judge, or analyze it. Don't attempt to modify it, reject it, or control it. Merely keep observing. Try only to become perfectly aware of all the body sensations that spring up and pass away.

Schedule:

Once or twice per day.

First week: 5 to 10 minutes.
Second week: 10 to 20 minutes.
Third week: 20 to 25 minutes.
Fourth week: 30 minutes.

Possible obstacles:

Your body will attempt to move. Parts of your body that you were never even aware of before this practice will appear to hurt or ache. But you must stay still, do not twitch or stretch. Keep your attention centered on bodily sensations.

You might fall asleep or begin to enter into the dream state. Retrieve your focus every time you become aware that it is drifting away. Do precisely the same if you become semi-conscious because a stream of thoughts has grabbed your attention.

The result:

Deep relaxation of both the body and the mind will occur. By continuously watching the rise and fall of all bodily sensations, your concentration is being trained and perfected as well.

The state you get after this practice is done is the perfect basis for all the other practices. Your awareness will be magnified to a state of deeper consciousness, analogous to a trance state.

With time, this body awareness will extend to daily activities as well. While taking a bath, dressing, eating, and walking, you will become aware of sensations in your body that you were previously completely unconscious of. You will have a better understanding of what's going on inside your physical and energetic body.

As a side-effect, you will notice that you will become aware if something is wrong in your body much earlier than what would otherwise be noticeable. A practitioner might sit with the wrong posture in a chair for multiple months before the pain starts to get noticed. However, with this practice, if you are wrongfully sitting in a chair, you will become aware of that minute pain, and you will be able to fix your posture accordingly.

Phase Three: The Art of Relaxation

Deep physical relaxation is a tremendously important ability to integrate into the student's mystical practice and life. Relaxing is precisely the opposite of stressing out. It is very beneficial to learn how to practice deep relaxation because many of the deeper meditations require the ability of deep physical relaxation.

Even if you feel that you are already relaxed, there's a possibility that you are not. In this practice, you will find tension in various muscle groups that was previously unnoticed.

To begin, you must use the posture that you've used in the previous practice. Although a student can theoretically achieve a deeper relaxation or trance state by lying flat on their back, this can also metamorphose into sleep or dullness. Therefore, unless the student has performed the previous phase by lying down, it is advised not to lie down for this practice.

Furthermore, it is advised to spend a few minutes doing the previous phase before beginning this practice. They are both connected and work in unison. However, when you are able to instantly recreate the state of deep stillness that occurs after the previous practice has ended, either by the act of posturing yourself in your usual meditative posture or by sheer will, then you no longer need to do this quick preparation.

Procedure:

1. Take a profound inhalation through your nostrils and as you exhale, sigh deeply. Assure that you breathe through the diaphragm because it will make the breathing deep and long, relaxing the musculature and the nervous system. Execute this step 10 times.

2. Notice any tensions within the body. By concentrating on that particular body part, you are stimulating the nervous system there, lessening the pressure. It will feel like a mild tingling in the body part you are focusing upon. Relaxing these areas will permit an increased blood flow, softening any tightness.

Using your power of focus, you are relaxing blood vessels and increasing the heat of that particular body part, which will activate the relaxation response.

You can relax even more by using your imagination. Try one of these methods:

a) Visualize the area you're attempting to relax and, with your intention, see it relax more and more;

b) Each time you exhale, drop the control of that area as if you were surrendering all the tension to God;

c) Imagine yourself massaging that area with your "astral hands";

d) Mentally say, while focusing on that area: Relax... Relax... I relax...

3. Feel yourself falling deeper and deeper. Imagine the sensation of falling down and down. Notice how your body seems to melt, relaxing more and more with each exhalation.

4. Notice a bright white light in your heart. This light is very soothing and relaxing. As you inhale, feel this white light expanding into your entire body, spreading from the heart upwards, towards the brain, and downwards, towards the feet. This white light bathes your whole body with radiant and relaxing energy.

5. Repeat step 4 five times or until you feel relaxed and refreshed. Do not let your awareness fade into a semi-conscious level, but keep it alert and focused.

6. Now that your body is relaxed and "sparkling white", imagine a horizontal clear-sky blue light at your feet as vividly as possible. Make this blue light as radiant as possible.

7. See this blue light moving gradually upwards, like a scanner, starting at the feet, making them extremely heavy and relaxed. Hold the visualization until the feet are so relaxed that you can barely feel them.

8. Slowly move the bright blue light upwards to your legs and calves. Maintain it there until all remaining tension dissipates.

9. Next, visualize the bright blue light moving further up towards the thighs. Let it remain there until all tension has fully disappeared.

10. Keep doing the same for all the other body parts: hips, buttocks, lower back, abdominal region, chest, upper back, arms, shoulders, and neck.

11. Finally, do the same for the head and the brain. Let them be completely relaxed, free of all tension.

12. When this bright blue "scanner" light reaches the top of the head, move it downwards, towards the feet.

13. Repeat this process over and over again, but faster and faster each time. After 10-15 rounds, it should move from the toes to the top of the head and back in two seconds.

14. Now execute it even faster, so fast that each round takes less than half a second.

15. Your body is so deeply relaxed at this stage that you couldn't even move it if you wished to. Bathe for a while in this pleasant feeling of deep relaxation. It is blissful and warm. Either you feel bodiless at this time, or a gentle fuzzy tingling permeates your whole body.

Schedule:

Once or twice per day.

First week: 30 minutes.
Second week: 40 minutes.
Third week: 50 minutes.
Fourth week: 1 hour.

Possible obstacles:

It is essential to develop the power of concentration while practicing deep physical relaxation. Do not allow your attention to wander from the region you are focused on to some random thought or imagery. Just like in the previous phase, smoothly bring it back if it drifts away from your conscious focus.

This technique can get so relaxing and deep that you lose consciousness, falling into a numb state. Do not allow that to happen. Stay extremely alert but relaxed. Your ability to concentrate and relax will improve each time you sincerely practice.

The result:

This practice will carry your relaxation and consciousness

further into the semi-conscious realm but with full conscious-ness.

You might feel your body drift, float, expand, diminish, contract, explode, implode, enlarge, separate, etc. You may also lose body-awareness of some particular parts, like the hands, arms, or legs.

It is possible, and even very likely, that you can relax the whole body to the point of feeling that it doesn't exist any-more, except for the head. The head and the brain will be the most challenging part to relax and let go of, but with per-severance and dedication, it shall be done.

Throughout each cycle, you can pause and observe how you feel. The previous practice has enhanced your ability to perceive and be cognizant of what's happening inside your body, sometimes even to the cellular level.

This practice is blissful and provides, as a side-effect, the equivalent of some hours of sleep for many practitioners. Consciously going deep into relaxation can do wonders for the body and the mind's recovery. Enjoy the pleasure and freedom that you will experience at the end of this practice.

After enough practice, this level of pleasurable deep relax-ation can be evoked anywhere at will, without the need for a comfortable and silent place or for the employment of any technique. All you need is to think of it, to remember the feeling of relaxation as vividly as possible. Take a deep breath and then heave a deep sigh, and the marvelous feeling of blissful relaxation will arise within you.

This will also help open the latent abilities within your psyche or allow you to perform profound affirmations to your subconscious mind.

Phase Four: Breathing & Vital Force

Before beginning this practice, try to replicate the relaxed state of the previous phase just by consciously and vividly remembering it.

By now, you should be capable of achieving a reasonable deep relaxing state just by the act of placing yourself in your regular meditation posture. This deeply relaxed state is tremendously important. If you can't bring about that state yet, you can do the previous phase for ten minutes right before starting this practice.

There is immense tension spread throughout the body, particularly in the diaphragmatic and abdominal areas, preventing a student from breathing correctly. But, after practicing the previous phase for the stipulated amount of time, these troubled areas should be cleared out at this time, facilitating both the breathing process and the flow of vital force.

Those students with anxiety, emotional problems, or stressful lives normally have their breathing process partially blocked with considerable muscular tension, developing deficient oxygenation and low vitality and energy.

Owing to that, in this phase, we will turn our attention towards the breath and the vital force, purifying our vital channels and the whole breathing process.

Procedure:

1. Sit in your normal posture and consciously bring about the deep relaxing state of the previous phase.

2. Visualize a bright white glowing sphere of energy at the coccyx.

3. Inhale and move the radiant white sphere of energy from the bottom of the spinal cord upwards until the top of the head through the spinal cord for a count of six (See the image below). You can use the traditional mantra *Om* or *Aum, Ram, Tao, El,* or any other of your choosing. Just make sure it's one-syllable only. We employ it merely for counting.

It is essential that the six counts are spaced correctly, with the same amount of time between them. This rhythm is vital and should not be neglected.

4. Exhale deeply for the same length as the inhalation (a count of six) while bringing the bright white sphere of energy from the top of the head towards the coccyx through the front of the body.

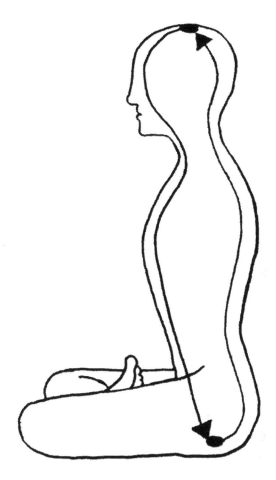

The breathing must be abdominal, expanding the abdomen during the inhalation and contracting it at the end of the exhalation. The navel will expand and contract towards the spine, respectively.

Schedule:

Once or twice per day.

First and second weeks: 10 minutes.
Third and fourth weeks: 15 minutes.
Fifth and sixth weeks: 20 minutes.
Seventh and eighth weeks: 25 minutes.
Ninth and Tenth weeks: 30 minutes.

Optional: Perform 10 minutes of Phase Three, each time, before practicing this phase.

At the end of this routine, remain in your chosen posture for five minutes to allow the effects to assimilate. Do not focus on anything in particular. Merely enjoy the sensations and observe.

Do not rush this phase. It will require some time to perfect it, but it will be worth it. A slower, deeper, and subtler breath prolongs life and reduces stress, anxiety, compulsive thinking, etc. It makes life more enjoyable, and it will improve your concentration tremendously.

Possible obstacles:

Do not strenuously force the mind nor overtax the lungs by taking the breathing process beyond your current limits.

Effort should be employed, but the practice must be easy and pleasant.

In the beginning, it might be slightly confusing and arduous, but given enough practice, the rhythmic nature of the breath in this practice will take a life of its own. Progressively, the lungs, the air pathways, and the mind will sing in harmony, making the whole process automatic and spontaneous, yet with full awareness. It will become simple, joyful, and even euphoric.

Keep your focus fixed in your practice, and do not let it wander. Your ability to concentrate will undergo a significant change. Breathing exercises require discipline and determination to master. When the pleasurable feelings arise, it will become much easier, and the tendency of the mind to disturb will soften dramatically with this practice.

The result:

Although it starts with breath control at first, the whole method will become subtler and subtler, ultimately leading the student to control the vital force and re-energizing it. The breath will become so long and subtle that it might even be entirely imperceptible.

It's probable that this practice will bring about many mystical experiences, and even euphoric and ecstatic states. Let them all occur, and naturally assimilate them in your bodily vehicle. Vitality and peace will ensue as well. Deep conscious breathing achieves many essential functions of the body, and it not only oxygenates the blood but also stores vital energy.

With sufficient practice, your whole body will start to vibrate with pleasure, causing the whole organism to come to life with an endless force and power never experienced before. The mystical energy is awakening in you.

Phase Five: Sacred Syllables

By this stage, the practitioner will be considerably familiar with the state of their mind, thoughts, bodily sensations, feelings, and emotions.

Once they begin practicing deep meditation, the mind will seem to rebel, as new unconscious fears, latent thoughts, forgotten memories, and out-of-character reactions during daily life may surface.

The peace and joy that have been acquired from the previous phases may seem to fade into the background because of the new, unanticipated strength of the mind.

We will employ the practice of mantra in this phase because it is perfect for calming the mind quickly and dissolving this unwanted disturbance while simultaneously increasing our ability to concentrate and abide in stillness. Many people swear by the use of some specific mantra, but we suggest that each student chooses one that fits their tendencies of mind.

Procedure:

1. Repeat that mantra mentally, over and over again, for the chosen amount of time. Every time you lose the mantra, merely come back to it. The speed or rhythm that you employ does not matter.

2. In the course of time, the mind itself will take the mantra,

and it goes on repeating these mental syllables automatically. You should then merely observe the mantra go on and on by itself.

After the meditation is over, stay in your current posture for 5 minutes resting. Don't do anything in particular, just rest.

With sufficient practice, the mantra might become fuzzy and nearly imperceptible, but you know it's still being chanted by the mind, subtly and non-vocally. You will perceive the mantra being chanted but as silence. Words cannot easily communicate this, but it is perfectly understandable to the student that sincerely practices it.

Schedule:

Once or twice per day for 30 minutes. You can do Phase Four before it for 10 minutes if it helps you become more focused and calm.

Duration: 2-6 months.

This practice requires much more time allocated than the previous ones because it is harder to master. Mastery of this method is vital. For many students, six months will not be sufficient.

Possible obstacles:

The number of times you will forget to chant the mantra will be endless. Should that happen, merely come back to inwardly chanting the chosen mantra. The mind will wander, but you will bring it back to a single point over and over again.

You may experience some irritability or impatience with this practice after some months of practicing it. To solve that problem, you can either reduce the time to 20 or 10 minutes, or practice only once daily.

This can also signify that you are being too soft with the practice. Remember that it is a concentration practice, and you must maintain the focus on the mantra, regardless of whether it's crystal clear, fuzzy, or extremely polished.

Don't hasten the process, but patiently keep practicing because the goal of Union with God is no superficial goal but a life-changing conquest.

The attainment of perfect concentration is possible but requires hard work. It is impossible to learn how to play the piano in one month; and the ability to consciously control attention and sustain it at a chosen point for an indeterminate amount of time is even harder. But it's worth every bit because the ecstasy of God awaits you.

The result:

As a consequence of this practice, your inner peace and silence will expand and grow naturally. Your daily activities and life will be embellished by profound stillness and serenity, even during strenuous activities.

Concentration will also become constant and effortless. In the long run, you will be able to use your ability of extreme focus whenever you wish, without needing any preparation.

Your mind will also develop a powerful mental, emotional and physical balance. The deep silence that emerges within after this practice is remarkable.

The breath will slow down dramatically with this practice, even to the point of nearly stopping completely. That's an indication that our metabolism is slowing down as a side effect of this practice. It's completely normal, and you don't need to analyze or be aware of it. It's a sign of deep purification as well.

Many energetic and mystical experiences can occur during and after this practice. Let them come, let them be, and let them go.

However, if you get elevated into a euphoric silence during this practice, remain there. Do not chant the mantra during these moments, but cultivate abidance in thoughtless awareness.

Phase Six: Energy Centers

Because of the serene state of mind achieved by the previous phases, the student can now open up their mind to the light of God from within.

This light has been called many names, such as Kundalini, Holy Spirit, etc.

Even if progress from this moment on might seem very slow, the student must not become disheartened. Mysticism does not bring immediate results. Those are in the realm of drugs, which then may also bring a giant fall afterwards, and no permanent change is seen. Mysticism is about lasting change, not magical trips.

The student doesn't possess the necessary self-analysis to gauge the level of their development. Any thoughts of instant enlightenment or instant results must be tossed out. Discipline and determination are required.

The attentive student should have discovered by now that they have the universe inside them. The macrocosm is in the microcosm.

This practice will be given in three levels. Only after completing the first level should the student attempt the second, and so on.

a) Hindbrain Center Focus

b) Midbrain Center Focus

c) Forebrain Focus

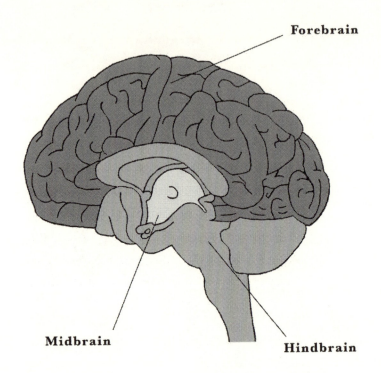

Hindbrain: The lower part of the brainstem (medulla oblongata, cerebellum, and pons).

Forebrain: The anterior part of the brain (thalamus, hypothalamus, and the cerebral hemispheres).

Midbrain: The middle of the brainstem (tegmentum and tectum).

Procedure:

a) Hindbrain center focus

Optional: Do Phase Four for 5 minutes.

1. Do Phase Five for 5 minutes.

2. Inhale deeply and move the vital force from the bottom of the spinal cord upwards to the area of the cerebellum in the hindbrain.

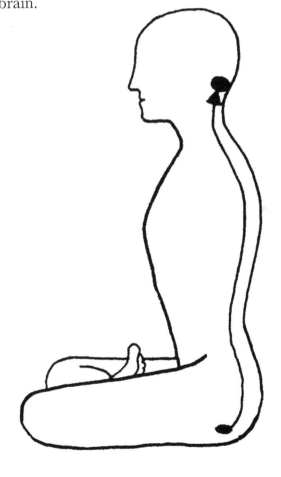

3. Once the vital energy is in the cerebellum, allow the breathing process to go on naturally.

4. Focus on that point to the best of your ability. Maintain the attention there.

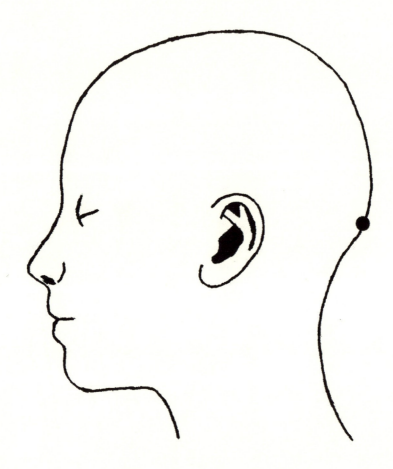

b) *Midbrain center focus*

The midbrain center is in the middle of the head. As it is hard for the majority of students to place their attention there, they should focus on the "third eye" instead because it is interconnected to the midbrain.

Optional: Do Phase Four for 5 minutes.

1. Do Phase Five for 5 minutes.

2. Inhale deeply and move the vital force from the bottom of the spinal cord upwards to the space between the eyebrows.

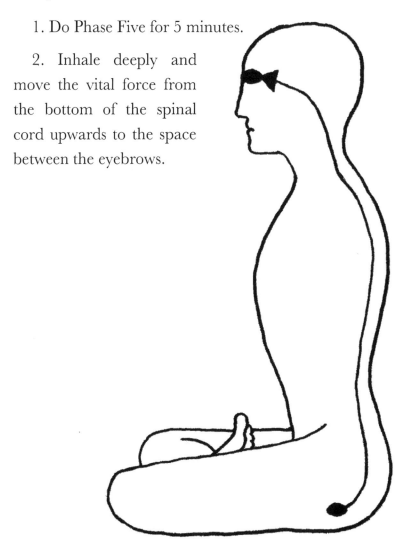

3. Once the vital force is in the space between the eyebrows, allow the breathing process to go on naturally.

4. Still the movement of your eyeballs. Fix your gaze on the space between the eyebrows to the best of your ability. Do not look forcibly inwards, and do not strain the muscles of the eyeballs. That will only give you a headache. Maintain the attention there.

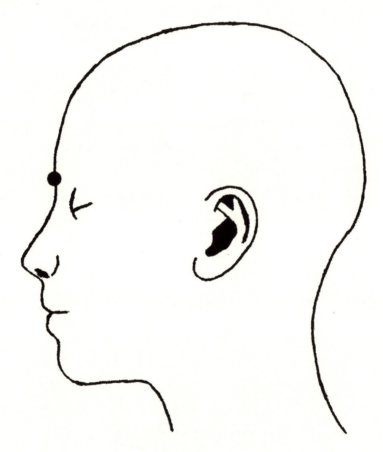

(Some practitioners feel this center more strongly by focusing one inch above the space between the eyebrows.)

C) Forebrain center focus

Optional: Do Phase Four for 5 minutes.

1. Do Phase Five for 5 minutes.

2. Inhale deeply and move the vital force from the bottom of the spinal cord upwards to the top of the head.

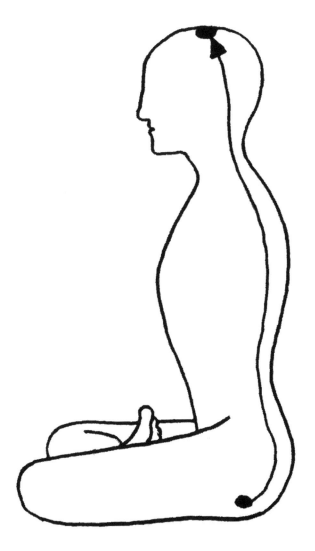

3. Once the vital force is in the top of the head, allow the breathing process to go on naturally.

4. Still the movement of your eyeballs. Fix your gaze on the space above the head. Do not look forcibly upwards, and do not strain the muscles of the eyeballs. If your eyelids open slightly during this practice, do not worry, it is expected. The eyes will become comfortable and steady with adequate practice. But remember never to strain them.

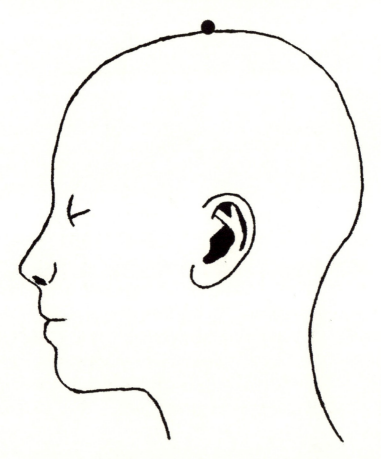

Schedule:

Once or twice a day for 20 to 30 minutes.

Practice *a)* (Hindbrain center focus) during the first month, and practice *b)* (Midbrain center focus) from then onwards. Once your concentration is stable there and you have experienced multiple periods of thoughtlessness, do practice *c)* (Forebrain center focus).

If at any time you experience adverse purification side effects from this (Forebrain center) practice, perform practice *b)* until you are comfortable again. Then you can practice *c)* again.

Possible obstacles:

The same obstacles of the previous phase (regarding concentration) will apply here, but instead of being for a mantra, they will be for the exclusive focus on an energy center. With that stated, this practice should be done after the ability to concentrate has been developed to a significant level in the previous phase.

Stilling the sight on the energy center b) and c) must be a progressive and natural process, without any strain. With adequate practice, you will be able to keep your gaze steadily without flickering. With sufficient practice, it will become second nature.

The focus on the designated energy center must be exclusive. The entire mind must be concentrated on the energy center, not allowing a single thought to arise.

Regardless of the strength of the student's intention, there will be days when the mind will be more dispersed than usual. If that becomes recurrent, there is little point in forcefully trying to control the mind. In this case, it is advised to do Phase Four and Five for 10 min each and then this phase for 10 minutes as well, before resting in the end for 5 minutes.

The result:

With adequate practice, as the student is able to control the restless mind successfully, periods of thoughtlessness will begin to arise. In the beginning, these periods will last just a few seconds, but after much practice, they will grow into minutes, and one day they will spread into daily life as well, infusing it with joy and serenity.

During this practice, it is possible that the student experiences visions, develops powers, feels the spiritual currents of vital force, or experiences tremendous ecstasy. The student can enjoy these as long as he doesn't become attached to them. "Eat the chocolate and savor it, but don't crave for more afterwards" should be the motto. There is no guarantee that any of these will occur, and it is likely that the student will only experience one of them. The degree and intensity of such an experience will depend on innumerable variables, such as the student's tendencies, pureness, etc. There is also the possibility that the student does not experience anything at all during the course of their mystical path. However, that does not indicate that they are not progressing.

Attempting to experience a vision forcefully or making arduous efforts to feel the vital currents, for instance, will only disturb the student's practice and mental state. The best state of mind should be one of letting these experiences come, if they come, by their own accord.

Optional Practice:

While practicing the Midbrain Center Focus technique, the student may experience the awakening of the so-called "third eye". This awakening may allow the student to see with their inner vision while performing the practices. If the student would like to expand on this inherent ability, they should follow the additional practice:

Awakening the Inner Vision

This additional practice can be performed right after the primary practice (or a few minutes later), or at any time during the day. It is for students who desire to go further and awaken their inner vision quicker. However, there are no guarantees that it will happen, as the mind and its characteristics differ for each student.

This practice stimulates the Midbrain center (third eye) to quicken its opening. The main practice also awakens the inner sight, but this extra gives it a boost. It must be done daily.

The student should execute it without expectations and with the greatest tranquility and peace. Anxiety or frustration will only fuel more stress and frustration, taking the student nowhere.

Procedure:

1. Sit in your standard meditation posture.

2. Close the eyes;

3. Do five deep breaths to soothe body and mind;

4. Start the Mystic Breath and do it for 3 to 5 minutes.

5. Next, center your attention on the space between the eyebrows while maintaining the Mystic Breath. When inhaling, visualize the universal golden energy coming from

the source of the Universe itself, accumulating between the eyebrows. When exhaling, see the third eye shining in bright golden light, as if it were the sun. You should feel a small pressure there, in the third eye.

6. Keep doing this for 10 to 20 minutes.

The intensity and flow of the energy will vary from practice to practice. So if the energy and intensity don't seem powerful enough in one day, it does not imply that something is going awry. All students should maintain their motivation and commitment regardless of the daily outcome.

As you go through this practice, you will verify that you may see some shapes and colors and can even hear some astral sounds. You should let these phenomena happen naturally without desiring to maintain them.

However, unlike in the primary practice, you can and should switch the focus of your attention towards these new phenomena that appeared, but with no force and without trying to maintain them. The attention should be steadily but calmly changed from the Mystic Breath, the space between the eyebrows and the visualizations, to the subtle phenomenon that appeared in your field of perception (such as spiritual light, but not exclusive to the field of subtle vision; it can be subtle sounds, subtle smells, etc.).

All students, essentially, without exception, will find that this alteration of focus is a highly volatile event in practice. When you attempt to change your attention to these subtle spiritual phenomena, they will disappear. With time and given sufficient practice, you will learn how to passively perceive these subtle phenomena, letting them grow and expand. Consequently, you will be able to actively focus on them and go deeper into absorptive states.

If these phenomena cease to manifest at any time, you must accept that without feeling frustrated. Resorting to the imagination to recreate them is prohibitive. These natural and subtle spiritual phenomena must appear on their own.

If either during the focus on the space between the eyebrows or after changing the focus to the subtle phenomena, you experience an immense sense of space or emptiness, as if you were in a void, you should remain there intentionless. This is a very advanced state beyond all spiritual manifestations.

Phase Seven: Subtle Noticing

In this phase, the student's focus is aimed towards the activity of the mind. In Phase Two, the student directed their attention to the arising and passing of bodily sensations, while in this phase, they'll do the same but for the arising and passing of everything in the mind.

As of now, the mind should be quite calm and controlled. All practices done during the previous months have made it pure, tranquil, and capable of having a stable focus. However, there will be times when the mind is still not under control. This is the perfect time to watch it and see which latent thoughts and subtle mental habits are holding the mind back from being entirely transparent.

This practice will show the student what lies beneath the surface, deep down in the unconscious. Some of the thoughts and imagery that will arise may be unexpectedly emotional or intimate to the student (i.e., childhood traumas). By taking this passive yet conscious approach, everything that is concealed that has not been erased by the active practices of the previous phases will now be illuminated.

Procedure:

1. Let the mind wander as it wishes, in any direction it desires.

2. Do not attempt to curb it. Don't inhibit any of its movements. Merely observe it.

3. When observing, do not identify with the contents of the mind. Let it wander as it wishes, regardless of what has captivated its attention. Watch these contents passively as if from afar.

4. Just impersonally watch the mind. Nothing more is required.

5. When there are neither thoughts nor anything to observe, remain in that emptiness, letting God absorb you.

Schedule:

Once, twice, or three times a day for 30 minutes.

Possible obstacles:

The student will notice that during the initial stages of their practice, they will constantly identify themselves with the unconscious flow erupting in the mind. Patience is a much-needed skill to conquer subtle and unconscious restlessness. Sitting or lying down with the eyes closed, having the mind wander out of control, and then getting up and thinking that one has practiced is foolish.

During this process of watching the apparent random flow of thoughts, there should be no self-judgment or self-criticism. There must be acceptance of whatever arises in the mind. Soon enough, the student will recognize that these

chaotic thoughts are not theirs and are merely randomly happening without any conscious intention or control.

This phase will also be the longest of all. It will take quite
some time to get used to being in the observer's position,
rather than losing oneself in subtle mental content. But the
most advanced phase of deep mysticism requires this discon-
nection from the mind in order to transcend one's individuality.

There may be many pleasurable and comfortable moments
during this phase, followed by unpleasant and uncomfortable
ones. Either way, the student should accept them just as
they come and go. Fighting, changing, rejecting, ignoring,
or suppressing whatever appears in the mind is not the solu-
tion. If the student attempts to do so, the mind will revolt
with much strength and will seem to generate a power that
it commonly does not possess, highly disturbing the Subtle
Noticing practice.

Never try to forcefully stop thoughts or coerce the mind
to be quiet, calm, or at peace. Doing that way will be impossible. We want the mind to be our butler and not our
slave that will kill us if we happen to forget to lock its chains.

The result:

The student must remember that our intention is to notice
the contents of the mind, whatever they may be. Visions,
lights, or any inner experience are also contents of the mind

and must be observed in the same way as if they were mere thoughts. If the student gets carried away by these experiences, they will lose focus.

Once the student has "integrated" and subsequently erased the identification with these emotional and hidden contents of the mind, a different form of quietude and joy will be recognized within. These two are different in quality when compared to the previous experiences of peace and joy, as they will be seen as non-arising but were only blocked by the mind. This is also because the student's psyche is now much purer and mature, capable of receiving the higher universal power.

After this intense purification, the student's mind will be much wiser and fresher, ready to tackle life with much more energy, wisdom, and pleasure. This liberated energy can then be utilized for a worthy purpose, such as a high creative output or even for supernatural pursuits.

As the subtle awareness of the contents of the mind is cultivated and developed, freeing the student from the mind's restraints, the nervous system will learn how to comfortably sustain serenity and pleasure while wholly engaged in the world.

Moments of inspiration and sagaciousness will become normal in the earnest student due to the high purification that the mind is going through. With access to deeper layers of universal intelligence, the intellect will also become brighter.

The pacification of mind, self-surrender, willpower, and mental focus that occur in this phase not only make the student ready for union with God (the ultimate goal) but also increase the individual output in standard competencies, such as giving a better ability to make and carry out decisions and the skill to deeply reflect on any subject with understanding, owing to the freedom from pointless and obsessive thoughts and habits.

When the student has gained proficiency in maintaining their mind steady, pure, and unattached to whatever arises and disappears, they will reach the absorption phase in God-consciousness. If the student remains in this state of union with God, they will realize their true Godly nature.

Phase Eight: Absorption

This phase culminates in the expansion of the previous phase to all of life.

Through the application of all these practices in each of the phases, the student has probably experienced union with God and has tasted the ecstasy of such union. This experience includes a phenomenological annihilation of multiplicity.

At this stage, the student is required to eradicate every remnant of individuality from their mind. If the multiplicity is still blurred, they must continue with their practice.

Every time the student achieves Absorption with God and assimilates these experiences into their life afterward, they will eliminate the toxic individualistic residues from their mind. Some of these residues are incredibly elusive and will take a while to erase completely.

When their union becomes permanent, the student realizes that everything is God. The world, the mind, every action, every person, and every object is God.

However, the world of appearances will remain exactly as it is. The body will still have to be taken care of. But no longer will the mystic be entangled in this world's deceptive stories and trapped in the roller-coaster of joy and grief.

The student realizes the unity of all of life, regardless of how diverse everything seems, finding a new way of approaching it. To others, unaware of the student's (now turned mystic) newly found inner light, their life might seem to stay the same. However, inside, the mystic is in total rapture and wisdom.

The unreality of time, although grasped, still governs the student's physical body life. They still have to live their life in this world by the clock.

There are various subtler planes to which the student can dislocate their consciousness and actually live a life there and interact with such beings. Their consciousness will learn how to be here and now in this world, and at the same time, in a subtler realm. All of these planes are still God, nonetheless. Everything is made of God-consciousness.

The mystic will assimilate such divine realization of union with God in their body and mind and express the beauty of God in this world.

Common Obstacles to Mystical Practice

All obstacles to a successful mystical practice come from inside. Although we have already specified which kind of obstacles may arise during the different types of practice, there are some that can happen to any practitioner, irrespectively of which type of meditation one is practicing: sleepiness, torpor, carnal passions, confused mind, dullness of mind, scattered thoughts, laziness, lack of intensity and surrender, self-judgmental, self-criticism, ill-will, anger, restlessness, perfectionism, impatience, lust, lack of proper sleep, lack of self-discipline, lack of motivation, lack of energy, lack of appropriate understanding about the mystical path, bodily-weakness due to inadequate nutrition, lack of trust in the teachings or the Master, etc.

Find out the distressing causes and eliminate them.

If you are excessively sleepy or lazy, breathe explosively through the mouth for ten rounds and then hold your breath for a count of 30. Then breathe normally, and you will be much more alert. If this doesn't work, stand up and dash cold water on your face. Desires and thoughts about what to do later in the day will also arise, and you should ignore them. If they are too loud, consciously let them be in full force until they settle. On the occasion that you lack motivation or surrender, you need to be inspired. Read some mystical and spiritual books and be encouraged.

All practitioners should try their best to avoid the company of those who are spiritually immature or those who try to drag them down, and should also stay moderate in speech, action, and food.

The biggest cause of failure in mystical practice is the láck of motivation, lack of fierce focus, lack of dispassion towards sense-pleasures and thoughts, and lack of understanding of what God really is and why He should be known. This understanding must arise in the practitioner, and it may be the case that this book sets that process in motion.

$$8$$

Mystical Experiences

ultiple practitioners have various mystical experiences during mystical practice. These experiences always depend on the practitioners' background, tendencies, disposition, and other factors.

Some practitioners will hear sounds without having to use their ears. Others will see visions without having to use their eyes. Some experience tremendous ecstasy, while others will have powerful deep metaphysical insights into the nature of God, reality, the cosmos, etc.

Countless different experiences can happen during mystical practice. We have already mentioned some in the Mystical Practice chapter.

If the practitioner sees a sudden flash of what can only be depicted as powerful Divine Light, they will be struck in awe and magnificence. They quiver in awe and devotion. The dazzling Divine Light is no ordinary light. It hits the mind with a mighty force, trembling it with love and complete absorption.

The practitioner can also experience a myriad of different visions and interact with multiple beings from subtler dimensions. Some will help a genuine student progress in the mystical path; others might be a distraction, to say the least. Your genuine intentions, the extent of your heart's immaculacy, and the "tests" that you must overcome to progress in the mystical odyssey are the rules on what sort of beings you will encounter.

Ecstasy is one of the most common and potent experiences as well. The experience of ecstasy can differ in potency according to how unimpeded the practitioner's body and mind are, and the place of concentration.

The most common and initial ecstasy will feel as if shivering energy went up the spinal cord, raising the hairs of the body (i.e., goosebumps).

This ecstasy will increase as the process of spiritual cleansing continues, and in due course, it will reach a full-blown mystical omnipresent rapture. This ecstasy is not felt only within the body but in the whole universe.

Fear of the beyond

All students are hungry for mystical experiences, but as soon as a powerful experience happens, they might experience immense fear.

This fear appears because they are about to go above mere body-consciousness, and their mind fears this abyss of uncertainty and mystery.

Human beings are accustomed to being restricted. When they go above these constraints through mystical practice, they feel like their ground which they were so used to, is no longer there.

Beyond Phenomena

Once the student arrives at the most advanced stage, their mystical practice will be on the vacancy of mind. It is in the emptiness without any shape that the God state is finally achieved. This is beyond all meditative experiences and mystical phenomena. It is verily Union with God.

9

Divine Abilities

ost human beings have latent abilities that may or may not be manifesting. The student may even be manifesting them unconsciously.

Some have exceptional gifts that enable them to sense future events or subtle energies, see non-physical beings and identical metaphysical phenomena. The manifestation of these abilities can occur voluntarily or involuntarily to any person.

Some practitioners might be interested in developing these supernatural abilities, or perhaps they already possess some extraordinary gift and would like to amplify it.

That is a gracious decision, but it is certain that an outward expression of power will never truly fulfill the sincere student as the quest towards God and subsequent Union will.

True divine abilities cannot be applied for personal gain or personal use. They purely flow through the mystic, using him as an instrument of the Divine. That's how real miracles are performed.

These divine abilities may or may not come. The student will try to use them, while the mystic will be empty of mind to allow the Divine to use him as an instrument. That is the contrast between the student and the mystic.

All the practices we've discussed can bring powers, but they are not for the attainment of powers. They are to enable the student to connect with a subtler dimension than the student is used to and to purify their nervous system and mind to allow the Divine Light of God to pour in, ultimately elevating them to achieve Union with God.

The student has to be cautious not to let these newly acquired mystical abilities become an obstruction. Their function is always to assist the journey, not interrupt one's search for God.

Consider the case of a man who aims to get to their homeland and is given a car with a full fuel tank to reach his destination more quickly. This man, who used to rely only on his legs, now had the opportunity to shorten the time of his trip and to do so more comfortably.

But instead of taking advantage of this help, he decides to take the gift that life has given him and spend all of the car's fuel drifting and racing against cars.

The main goal of returning to his homeland became secondary, seemingly abandoned. Now, in this man's mind, all he could think about was how to use the automobile to have fun and pursue futile activities that are no more than wasteful efforts.

As might be expected, after some time, the car will inevitably run out of gas. Unfortunately, only then will this man become aware of how tremendous the opportunity he had in his hands actually was. He could have arrived in his homeland much more rapidly than by foot, but having wasted the gas, he has to go back to walking.

To conclude, the student must let these divine abilities be the embodiment of divinity in the body and mind, without trying to derive personal benefit from them, but allowing them to express themselves in whatever situation they arise.

10

Out-of-Body Exploration

ountless mystical traditions employ out-of-body exploration as a useful mystical practice. Truth be told,
exploring subtle realms through out-of-body practice
can be a great tool in the student's arsenal, and regardless
of all the esoterism and complications attributed to it, the
whole methodology is quite simple and can be boiled down
to triggering an automatic "out-of-body reflex" built into
the mind.

Everyone can achieve out-of-body projection given sufficient and adequate training because this reflex is inherent
to all human beings. However, three crucial conditions
need to be addressed to induce such reflex while entirely
conscious.

Instructions:

Condition #1. Being capable of achieving a state of deep relaxation while staying awake.

The practice of Phase Three achieves this condition. If you desire to have out-of-body projections, you should practice "The Art of Relaxation" for one hour until you can consistently enter into a state where your body is asleep and your mind is awake.

With sufficient practice, you will be capable of reaching a state of deep relaxation in less than ten minutes, with nearly no effort at all.

Condition #2. Being capable of shifting your consciousness to an out-of-body point.

The practice of Phase One accomplishes this condition. You should practice "Attention with Focus on Space" (or on a distant point 30 cm in front of your body) for at least 30 minutes until you can enter into a state where your attention is so sharp and single-pointed that you can actively shift to out of the body.

If this is not the case, we can offer a different approach to fulfill condition two by using the sense of touch through active imagination. It works under the same principle. The fundamental is shifting your point of consciousness from behind the physical eyes, where it has been all your life, to outside your physical body.

Touch Sense through Active Imagination

This technique involves using the sense of touch by actively imagining that you are climbing a rope out of the body. It is a quite well-known technique in out-of-body projection circles.

It is one of the best for projecting out of the body, and it fits this condition number two perfectly by providing a focal point of consciousness to the exclusion of all other thoughts and mental images, and by serving as a potent visual indication to the mind that the consciousness in this body wants to project out of it (as a rope usually means we want to climb away from where we currently are).

By applying this technique, you will begin to feel vibrations. When vibrations occur, do not start to rope-climb, but allow them to happen without trying to superimpose some technique on them. By consciously soaking in these vibrations, the projection reflex will spontaneously occur without needing to do anything about it. They can occur on a particular body part or the whole body. Their intensity varies and can go from a simple buzzing to a gigantic pulsing.

You may feel fear and be somewhat anxious when these vibrations occur, but don't fight them off. Should the fear or nervousness overcome you, the projection will fail. Because it's a new process and a sensation that you are not used to experience in your body, these reactions are normal. Your heart will beat furiously at first, but it will become natural once you experience projection multiple times.

To make the projection happen naturally, only the three conditions mentioned in this chapter need to occur. Consistent practice of what will be explained in condition number 3 will awaken the spiritual current of vital force, and then only condition number one and two are required to trigger the out-of-body reflex.

Procedure:

After being able to feel the spiritual currents by having fulfilled condition number three (as it will be explained below) and having achieved a deeply relaxing state by fulfilling condition number one:

1. Become aware of your non-physical arms and hands.

2. Imagine yourself rubbing your non-physical hands together until you can clearly feel them.

3. Imagine a firm rope hanging from above your head (if you are sitting) or above your heart (if you are lying down).

4. Grab the rope with your non-physical hands. Become aware of the rope's texture using your touch sense imagination skills.

5. Climb hand over hand up the rope. Pull the rope towards you with one hand while the other is reaching out, just like you would do by climbing a physical rope with your

physical hands. Feel the texture of the rope when you are climbing it with your hands. For most students, this "feeling" of the texture will have a more powerful effect than just purely using the attention to focus on a point outside the body. Use your imagination and your subtle sense of touch to the best of your ability. The more real the rope's texture is, the higher the probability of having a successful out-of-body projection.

Using this rope technique grants a much gentler means of getting out of the body because you are feeling yourself literally getting out of your body rather than through pure visualization or concentration. This process engages the motor skills that are instinctively associated with physical motions.

6. Maintain this process for as long as possible, but do not tense your physical body or muscles. This is a mental action, and any tension will nullify your chances of projection. Stay centered on what you are doing, and don't let your mind wander.

If you practice lying down, it is best you don't do it on your sleeping bed. This is because you have programmed your body and mind to fall asleep in your bed, so it will make it really difficult.

Condition #3. Have the spiritual current of vital force already awaken in the energetic body.

The practice of Phase Four achieves this condition. You should practice "Breathing & Vital Force" for 30 minutes every day until you can vividly feel the spiritual currents within your spinal cord and brain.

As you practice controlling the breath, there may be an automatic tension of muscles. To prevent this from happening, always keep checking your muscles for tension and relax as necessary.

On the whole, these three conditions will enable the student to consciously project out-of-body. By practicing the primary mystical practices, each student will naturally acquire the ability to project out-of-body, given enough time. It will not happen on the first try, but be tenacious.

You can start attempting to project your consciousness out of the body right off the bat without having mastered the manifold phases in the primary practices.

1. Do Condition number 1 to the best of your ability for 30 to 60 minutes.

2. Do Condition number 2, either the standard version or the "Touch Sense through Active Imagination" to the best of your ability for 20 to 30 minutes or until you experience the projection-reflex.

3. Get out of the body.

It boils down to inducing a deep trance (condition 1) and performing the exit technique (condition 2). Both these conditions require the awakening of the spiritual current of vital force (condition 3) to be executed perfectly.

Possible obstacles and Tips:

Remain as alert and aware as possible during the whole preparation, and do your best not to slip into the dream state.

Rapid heart rate, strong falling sensations, and vibrations are all indications that the projection reflex is about to occur. 95% of the time, the rapid heart rate is an energetic symptom connected to the heart center, rather than your actual physical heart having a tachycardia. Do not hold yourself back and persist with full awareness.

You might feel acute pressure in your heart or solar plexus. That is normal, and don't worry. Nothing bad will happen to you. You can instantly come back to your body after projecting if you desire.

The main trick is getting your physical body asleep while staying awake. It is a tough mental habit to break, but one that you must get into the habit of doing. Once the body is asleep, the projection reflex will occur.

The best time to practice is during the daytime. If you practice at night when you go to sleep, you will fall asleep.

You also need to have a strong intention of wanting to project whenever you practice "Out-of-Body Exploration".

Maintain that strong intent to phase out of physicality present.

There is a very thin line between excessive and insufficient concentration. If your focus is weak, you start meandering and risk falling asleep; if your focus is too strong to the point of forcing, you will lose your relaxation.

Fundamentally, your state of mind must be one of permitting the non-physical reality to arise in your sphere of perception rather than you forcing to go there.

There are commonly resistant layers of conditioning that prevent students from successfully projecting. By practicing as laid out in the "Mystical Practice" chapter, the conditioning will be purged.

Right when the student is on the verge of exiting the physical body, they may experience different intense phenomena, such as weird movement sensations, auditory hallucinations of all forms, and visions. A continuous falling sensation similar to the sensation experienced when falling asleep, but more intense and prolonged, can also be experienced.

The student must ignore them and maintain the focus on projecting. These sensations terminate as soon as the student leaves their body. Everything will be peaceful and silent as soon as one's consciousness is out of the physical body.

By managing to project out-of-body, the student will be able to interact with other beings in other realms, gain new insights, visit any place in the Universe, develop extrasensory abilities and have powerful mystical experiences by having a direct connection with the subconscious mind, without the usual blockages from the conscious mind of the waking state. There are also other multiple benefits that hinge on each student's predispositions.

Nonetheless, the student should not forget that out-of-body exploration is an additional practice that doesn't replace the main practices, nor will it take the student towards Godly Union. It is beneficial for inspiration and acquiring new wisdom about the Universe and the manifested cosmos, but it can likewise become a trap, as was explained in the chapter "Mystical Experiences". Sooner or later, the student will have to go beyond all phenomena.

11

Infusing Divinity

The student of mysticism doesn't have to separate their mystical practice from their daily life. They can and should unite both, therefore turning all common and mundane tasks into a mystical practice.

The possibilities are endless, and we will give the example of two of them:

Conscious Eating

Eating food does not need to be an unconscious and instinctive activity. If the student energetically charges their meal with intention and eats it fully consciously, they will reap significant benefits. Should the student decide that they want to stop eating their food mechanically and stop overthinking during meals, they should follow this practice.

Procedure:

1. Choose a noble intention. It can be an increase in motivation to practice, an increase in concentration, a growth of surrender, or anything that helps you on the path of mysticism.

2. Sit in front of the dish you are going to eat while keeping that intention clear in your mind.

3. Look at the plate with the most focused concentration and intention you can achieve, and attempt to embody your intention into the food through imagination. You can place your hands in a blessing manner above the food if you prefer, to help to increase the intention, but doing it only mentally works as well. See a luminous golden energy coming out of your heart and expanding in the direction of your hands, and then towards the food, blessing it with your noble intention. See it charging the food and water. Do it for 30 seconds.

4. Next, slowly eat the impregnated food in total silence but with awareness, and with the certainty that your intention is passing from the food towards your physical and subtle bodies. Remain conscious and ignore thoughts.

This process not only strengthens your chosen intention but purifies your food as well. If you cook your own food, you can and should charge the food while cooking it.

In the case that the food you are eating is of animal origin, you should express your gratitude towards the beings that provided it, and if you are eating their meat, you can ask God to provide them with a better reincarnation. If the food is of plant origin, you can express your gratitude towards nature and mother Earth. Every time you are grateful for your food, you are cultivating devotion and surrender, which help open the doors of your heart, which in turn helps your mystical practice as well.

It is important to highlight that for this practice to work, your confidence in doing it, your trust in the process, and your concentration ability must be strong. Furthermore, don't eat in a hurry and eat the whole food; nothing should be left over.

Purifying Bath

The student can also apply the same principle of making daily life a mystical practice when taking a bath.

Taking a bath is a phenomenal metaphor for cleansing and purifying not only the physical body but also the psyche. The ritual of Purifying Bath can also eliminate excess of energy that the student has accumulated if the student's body has been charged with much more energy than it can handle due to the efficacy of the mystical practices referred to in this book.

Although both the bath and the shower are equally effective, we suggest the student takes a shower so that running water can be metaphorically employed as a purifier of negative energy and thoughts.

Procedure:

1. Be entirely conscious during the bath or shower. Like consciously eating, this mundane activity must be infused with focus, consciousness, and silence, transforming it into a mystical practice.

2. As the water runs from the shower (or from the bath tap), visualize it cleaning your mind as if each drop of water was full of purifying light and energy capable of cleaning negative thoughts and a divisive and egocentric mind.

3. When applying the shampoo or the shower gel as you wash your hair or body, visualize all the stress, thoughts, and psychological fatigue being absorbed by the foam, leaving your mind and energy clean.

4. Next, turning the water on again, as it cleans the foam away, visualize all those negative energies and thoughts being washed out with the foam.

To wind up, instead of merely taking a typical shower and cleaning the body, the student cleans their mind and energy as well.

By creating this routine, students will experience not only the benefits of having a cleaner and purer mind and body, but they will also subconsciously implant the intention to always be conscious.

Note: Salt is an excellent aid that can be used while showering or taking a bath. Being a natural physical and energetic purifier, if the student applies a powerful intention of purification as they did with the water and the foam mentioned earlier in this chapter, the same subtle cleansing result will ensue. Salt works wonderfully against negative energy and entities due to its inherent cleansing properties. By gently washing the body with salt, it will absorb all negative energy within the student's body and mind. Subsequently, the student should wash their body with warm water, cleaning the salt from the body.

12

Mystical Amulets

Since ancient times, amulets have been associated with mysticism. They have become the story of legends and fairy tales.

Apart from serving only as aesthetic props, the motives that lead to their use are varied: protection, power, invincibility, concentration, luck, health, money, success, fame, connection to a specific being or beings, identification with a particular mystical group, identification of a specific degree or position within a mystical group, etc.

The importance given to amulets in the various mystical traditions is surely notorious, often to the point of neglecting real inner work through mystical practice. In many of these groups, each student must possess such a token and carry it with him at all times, for different reasons according to each tradition or group.

This approach is not ideal for those on the quest for union with God, but it can certainly help, even if only through the placebo effect. This placebo effect is very strong, and it scientifically proves that believing in something can actually provoke changes in yourself. This belief must not be only on the conscious surface level but also on the subconscious level.

Millions of different shapes can be used: rings, bracelets, pendants, earrings, piercings, coins, medals, etc. The student should pick one that resembles the intention and desire they want to give it the most.

Procedure:

This process is not different from the process of impregnating food with an intention.

1. After choosing your amulet, put it in your hands and gaze at it intensively, charging it with the intention you want it to symbolize and emanate.

If you want it to serve as a concentration enhancer so that whenever you look at it, your concentration dramatically increases, you need to make that object the mental embodiment of concentration. Visualize that all concentration-energy that exists within the Universe is coming together and charging your amulet.

2. Keep charging it for 5 to 10 minutes every day for as long as you can. If one day you look at it naturally and suddenly feel an immense ability to concentrate, then the impregnation of the amulet is concluded. You don't need to charge it anymore.

From then on, use it whenever you need to dramatically increase your concentration (i.e., during mystical practice).

You can create as many amulets as you desire and give them as many different intentions as you wish (but never charge the same amulet with different intentions).

Do not fall into the trap of becoming attached to the amulet, believing that without it, you cannot do whatever ability you have impregnated it with. After serving its purpose, the amulet should be discarded to prevent the student from becoming overly attached to it. This also prevents the student from believing that in the case of losing it, the student would lose the ability or effect the amulet was having. Despite all external aids, every student must know that ultimately, every change or ability comes from within.

SECTION 3

New Horizons

13

The Gift of Giving

An essential component of spiritual development is when the student provides service and help to others without wanting or needing to gain anything in return. No thoughts of self-gratification should occur.

Without this selfless service, there can be no true advancement in civilization because people will have profit in mind instead of genuinely helping others.

Although there are some exceptions, many people will not help others without anticipating something palpable in return.

During the student's inner journey, they may become aware of help coming from subtle spheres of life. Those inner beings are continually helping sincere students by providing them with insights, wisdom, energy, inspiration, teachings, etc., precisely like a living Master would do. Genuine Masters provide selfless help to all their disciples because they wish that their students and all of humanity raise their consciousness to higher states. This new higher consciousness would enable humankind to also enjoy a life of peace, love, sagacity, and eternity.

One of the perfect examples of a selfless Mystic that performed divine service to humanity is Jesus Christ. The preconceived idea that the Mystic is cold, distant, and rigid is only a foolish conviction.

Selfless help can be offered in various ways, ranging from teaching about something beyond everyday life to helping build some noble infrastructure or mission, or even by providing financial assistance.

Mystical practice, when merged with selfless service, will help the student develop surrender, devotion, and unconditional love, which then make greed, materialism, egocentricity, and cupidity disappear entirely.

In the present day, everyone witnesses self-interest being placed above selfless service in the ostensibly implacable race to accumulate financial and material wealth, fame, and power, all fully motivated for egoic benefits.

All students must be aware that selfishness is one of the most severe impediments to mystical development and cleaning karma. They should, therefore, live their lives with total respect for all life forms and show unconditional help towards others when appropriate, helping them to progress in their mystical path, even if they are unaware of the fact that they are in one. All touches of love elevate not only students' lives but the whole universe.

14

Supreme Devotion

Devotion to God is as vital in the path of the mystic as actual mystical practice. In fact, union with God can be achieved through total and absolute devotion on its own, while Union with God through mystical practice needs devotion, otherwise, the practitioner will not succeed. A continuous flow of surrender and love to God and a desire to know who He really is in His core is vital.

Through mystical practice and surrender, the student's mind will become freer from the sheer weight it has been carrying for a long time, consequently enabling the student to be more joyful and less beaten by the world's tribulations, and to effortlessly and naturally develop compassion towards others.

This compassion will then allow the student to do legitimate selfless service, which in turn originates even more devotion, surrender, compassion, and joy. While the student is on the path towards becoming free, they are also able to offer more to the world than before; they are capable of offering true light to the world.

In exchange for this blessed emancipation from individuality and for the emergence of deep joy and silence within, the student is compelled to go out and emanate them to the world, according to the student's inclinations and the type of activities they like to do. Their choices in life will switch to be more in line with their and others' well-being, coming from a much deeper level within.

For this to happen and to succeed in the mystic's path, the student's longing for God is what is needed at first. Then comes action through mystical practice, allowing the student to see that they can experience and authentically know God, sparking the desire to know God even more. This ardent love for God is the nucleus of every mystical path.

It is in the hands of each student to decide whether to know God or not. It is the willingness to do mystical practice and study genuine mystical teachings that will take the student nearly all the way to God. Then, in the end, only true ardent love and devotion to Him will take the student through the final step.

That logging that the student feels to know God is verily God. That ecstasy the practitioner experiences during mystical practice is verily God. That omnipresent Godly-consciousness of unity that is experienced by the mystic is verily God.

The journey of devotion is progressive, not an immediate occurrence. With ongoing honest mystical practice and surrender, the student's legitimate longing for God will make them one with God. Devotion is truly loving God as oneself.

15

The Mystical Life

During the course of this text, it has become evident to the reader that it has been because of the scarcity of genuine understanding that today's world has been harmfully going away from God, from freedom, and from divine joy towards dogma, ignorance and excessive materialism, fueled by the blind mind.

As more beings on this planet begin to recognize their inner immortal self, an expansion of humanity's collective consciousness will gradually occur, which then becomes the impetus for yet more beings to awaken.

Both for their own benefit and of this whole process, students must direct all their energy and efforts to discover the magnificent nature of God, the infinite God-consciousness.

This discovery comes from genuine devotion and mystical practice and not from intellectual conjectures. Discussions about God, consciousness, and reality are only physical manifestations of mental chatter. Students must stick to their first-hand experience and not to conceptual speculation. The reader must experience what is mentioned in this book through mystical practice instead of merely believing in it. The mystical practice is thus self-validating.

Once we have awakened, we have the opportunity to begin to operate from the infinite potential living within us. Since everything that exists is manifested from that, which is God, which is us, we are capable of manifesting from that immeasurable source of life within us.

Only when the true essence of who we are becomes known to all of us, can we, as humanity, turn away from the darkness of the past towards the light of the present. Then and only then can the whole cosmos finally become a place of harmony, peace, and happiness for all living beings. Genuine devotion and mystical practice make the path of the Mystic.

Without exception, every being in this universe will have to embark on this sacred path back towards the Divine. That is our ultimate destiny.

No time should ever be wasted. The student must someday transcend the cycle of rebirth, being absorbed by the glorious ecstasy of God. Life will still bring its challenges and upsets because as long as we are on this Earth, the dichotomy of life will be present. But inside, the mystic is wholly immersed in God, eternally perfect.

Epilogue

As we have observed during the whole of this work, this book is not intended to present the means to seek after material abundance, but it fulfills the intention of assisting students in finding their way back to God. The student's opinion about mysticism has undergone a distinguishable recontextualization, and we wish that they will at no time deteriorate or forget this ancient wisdom by falling prey once more to the embellishments of material life. Mysticism will not be regarded as sheer nonsense anymore but as the path back towards the source of life.

Want to read more books like this? Show your feedback with a sincere review, or send an email to the author at mysticsarom@gmail.com, telling him what you thought about the book and what you'd like to see in new books (more mystic, occult and spiritual content, sharing more knowledge regarding practices, divine abilities, metaphysical explorations, etc.).

www.sacredmystery.org

Publications

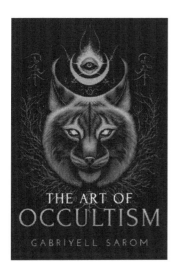

The Art of Occultism

The Secrets of High Occultism &
Inner Exploration

The Art of Magick

The Mystery of Deep Magick &
Divine Rituals

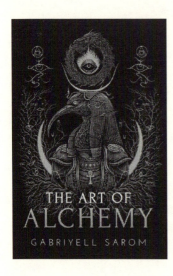

The Art of Alchemy

Inner Alchemy & the Revelation of the
Philosopher's Stone

Subscribe to Gabriyell Sarom's Newsletter and receive the book:

Divine Abilities:
3 Techniques to Awaken Divine Abilities

www.sacredmystery.org

Suggested Reading

- ### *Christian Mysticism*

A Course in Miracles by Helen Schucman

A full mystical guide from novice to advanced. We suggest it for those who are acquainted with the Christian terminology.

- ### *Eastern Mysticism*

Kundalini Exposed by SantataGamana

A powerful book with genuine depth and wisdom concerning Union with God and the vital force.

- ### *Western Mysticism*

Initiation into Hermetics by Franz Bardon

A classic text to become familiar with western magic and mysticism. It contains a practical guide.

- ### *Mysticism & Philosophy*

The Hermetic Philosophy of Ancient Egypt and Greece by Three Initiates

The essence of the teachings of Hermes Trismegistus.

Made in the USA
Las Vegas, NV
10 August 2024

93641849R00081